Boats

Paul Stickland

MATHEW PRICE LIMITED

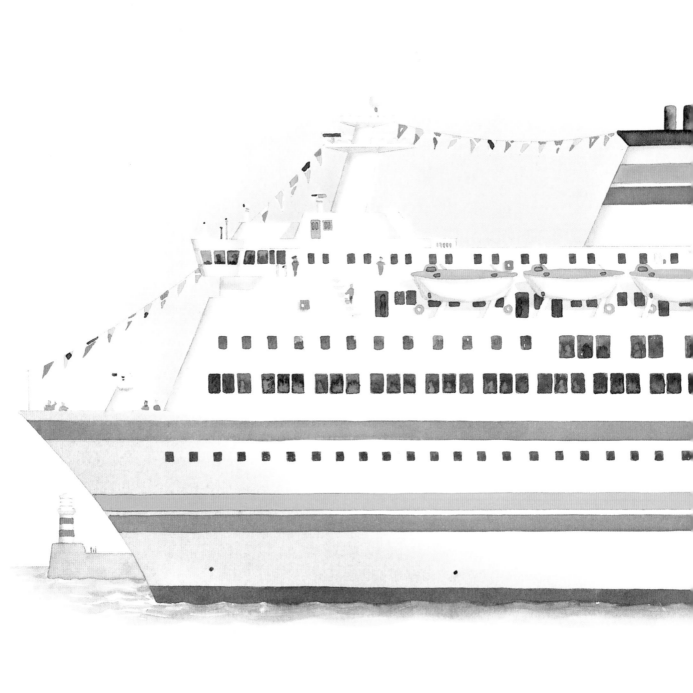

Ferries take cars and trucks and passengers across the water.

The captain of this FERRY must be able to see as much as possible as he manoeuvres this huge ship in and out of the harbour, so all the controls are up on the bridge, right at the top of the ship.

BRIDGE

LIGHTHOUSE

The flashing light at the top warns ships the coast is near.

LIFEBOATS

These boats can rescue everybody on board if it is necessary.

This ferry will take you and your car across the water. You drive your car on to the ferry, get out and then you can climb upstairs on to the higher decks, where there are cafés and shops to enjoy whilst you are travelling.

There are many levels, or decks, on a ferry, with stairs between. On some decks you can walk around the outside. It can be very windy.

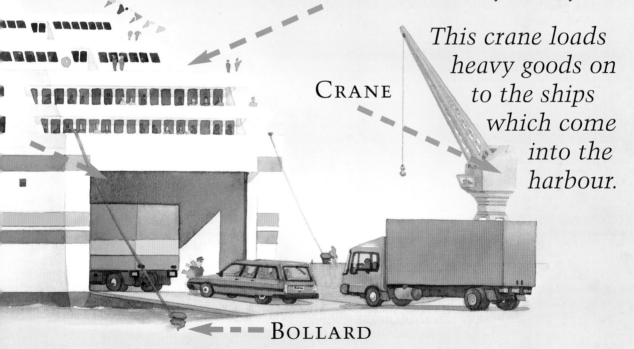

This crane loads heavy goods on to the ships which come into the harbour.

CRANE

BOLLARD

When the ferry comes in, big ropes are thrown down and tied to the bollards. Then the captain lowers the great metal door so that cars and trucks may drive on or off.

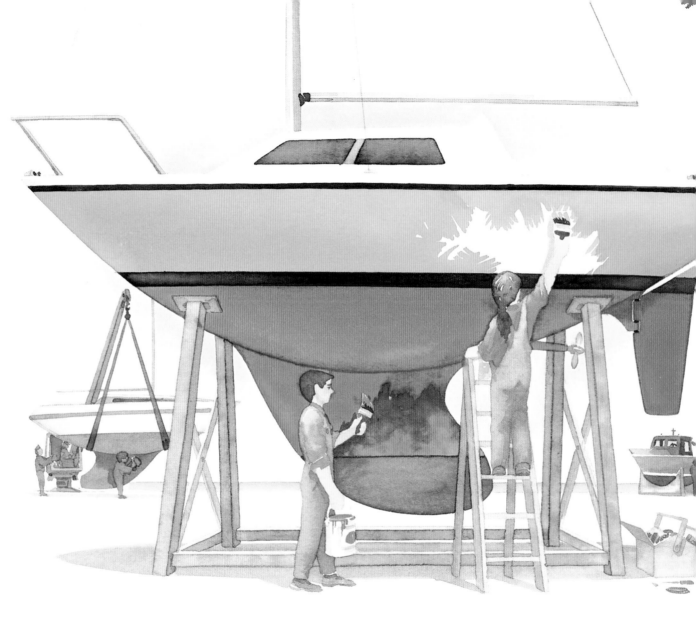

All boats need repairing and repainting
from time to time.

A rowing boat is pulled through the water with oars.

The body of a YACHT is called the hull and the only way to repair or paint it is to lift it out of the water with a crane and place it in a cradle on the harbourside. You might have to do this every year.

PROPELLOR

KEEL

It is very heavy and keeps the boat upright when you are sailing.

Yachts are wind-powered but all have an engine and propellor, in case the wind drops.

RUDDER

for steering the boat.

ROWING BOAT. *You could go on great holidays on a river. People who live near rivers sometimes use rowing boats for everyday travel.*

OARS
made of wood.

ROWLOCKS
to hold the oars.

PICNIC

LIFEJACKET

ROWER
faces backwards, pulling the dinghy through the water.

WATCH THAT DOG!

The power for a rowing boat comes from the rower, who has a pair of wooden oars. They pivot in rowlocks on either side, with thin curved blades to pull through the water.

A powerboat has two engines to make it go very fast. In the cabin there is a kitchen, four beds and a shower.

A hydrofoil is a high-speed passenger ferry. The boat lifts up as it skims across the surface of the water.

Safety is very important at sea, all of these children are wearing lifejackets to keep them afloat if they fall overboard.

STEERING WHEEL

RADAR

POWERBOATS *are usually made from plastic but inside they are made of wood. They are carefully designed with beds, a kitchen, dining room, shower and toilet.*

A powerboat is just for fun. They usually have two very powerful engines, which will propel the boat at over 50mph, using an enormous amount of fuel.

HYDROFOILS work well on calm water but they are not so good on a stormy sea.

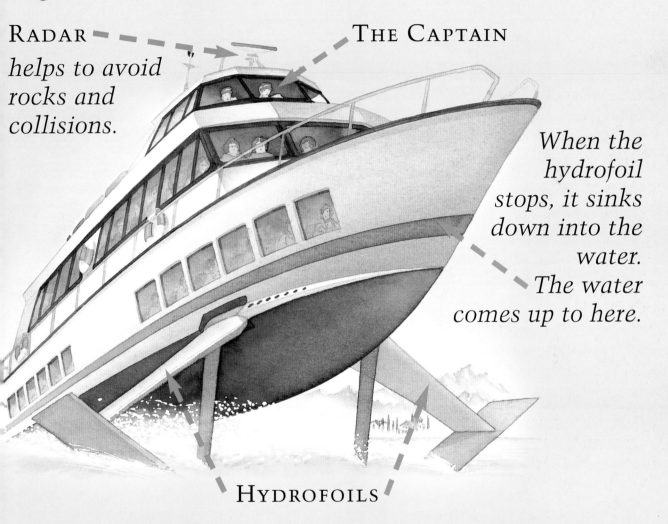

RADAR helps to avoid rocks and collisions.

THE CAPTAIN

When the hydrofoil stops, it sinks down into the water. The water comes up to here.

HYDROFOILS

It is quite difficult to push a large boat through the water. Fitting hydrofoils underneath makes the boat rise up clear of the water, so it can then travel at high speed.

This is an old wooden sailing ship.
The more sails it has to catch the wind
the faster it goes.

A liner is very difficult to steer, so a powerful tug pulls it into the harbour.

Only powered by wind and the hard work of the sailors, ta.
ships used to travel thousands of miles across the oceans.

Sailors had to climb right up the masts to put up the sails.
Very scary in a stormy sea with
the ship leaning over, the waves
crashing over the deck and
the wind howling
through the rigging.

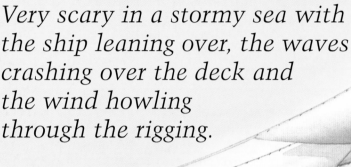

RIGGING

FIGUREHEAD
This was usually
a model of a
beautiful woman.

BOW

The ANCHOR *is lowered on a*
heavy chain down to the seabed,
when the ship is moored.

STERN

A vast LINER will need the help of very powerful tugs to tow it into harbour. Even though it is much smaller, the tug's huge engine allows it to pull the liner safely into the dock.

BRIDGE

ABINS

The captain on the bridge of the liner speaks to the captain of the tug by radio.

RADIO MAST

The Plimsoll LINE:
Water comes up to this level when the liner is fully loaded.

STEEL HAUSER, *very strong.*

This oil tanker is empty. When it is full it is so heavy it takes an hour to stop.

The petrol and diesel we use in our cars is made from oil. Oil is pumped from under the ground and carried all over the world in huge TANKERS like this one.

This shape on the hull of the ship helps it cut through the water and stops the ship rolling in heavy seas.

PROW

These dinghies are sailing a bit too close to the tanker.
It is very slow and difficult to steer, so they have to get out of its way.

Some tankers are nearly a mile long and the crews use bicycles to get from one end to the other.

Fifty people live and work on this ship for many months at a time.

FUNNEL
A giant exhaust pipe for the tanker's enormous engines.

PLIMSOLL LINE

The oil goes in here.

A tanker is like a giant metal box. When it is empty and the tanks are full of air the ship sails high in the water. When it is pumped full of oil, it sinks much lower in the water, down to the plimsoll line.

How,
Why,
What For

What's it for?

How does this float?

What's wrong?

This isn't a working boat, so what's it for?

What are these tyres for?

What are these people doing?

How do these yachts stay up even when they're leaning over?

The **Answers** Page

 This dinghy is full of air so it makes it light enough to float.

 This is a luxury yacht for cruising on holiday.

 To have fun exploring.

 They are fenders, to protect the tug in case bumps against the doc or another boat.

 This boy isn't wearing a life-jacket.

 These people have to their sailing boat on to trailer. This makes it easier to take the boat out of the water.

 The keel under the water is so heavy it keeps the boat upright

This edition first published in the UK 2004
by Mathew Price Limited
The Old Glove Factory, Bristol Road
Sherborne, Dorset DT9 4HP, UK

Designed by Douglas Martin
All rights reserved
Printed in China
ISBN 1-84248-115-0